DYLAN and COLE SPROUSE

Amie Jane Leavitt

P.O. Box 196
Hockessin, Delaware 19707
Visit us on the web: www.mitchelllane.com
Comments? email us: mitchelllane@mitchelllane.com

Mitchell Lane PUBLISHERS

Printing   2   3   4   5   6   7   8   9

A Robbie Reader
Contemporary Biography/Science Biography

Albert Einstein	Albert Pujols	Alex Rodriguez
Aly & AJ	Amanda Bynes	Brittany Murphy
Charles Schulz	Dakota Fanning	Dale Earnhardt Jr.
Donovan McNabb	Drake Bell & Josh Peck	Dr. Seuss
Dylan & Cole Sprouse	Henry Ford	Hilary Duff
Jamie Lynn Spears	Jessie McCartney	Johnny Gruelle
LeBron James	Mandy Moore	Mia Hamm
Miley Cyrus	Philo T. Farnsworth	Raven-Symone
Robert Goddard	Shaquille O'Neal	The Story of Harley-Davidson
Syd Hoff	Tiki Barber	Thomas Edison
Tony Hawk		

Library of Congress Cataloging-in-Publication Data
Leavitt, Amie Jane.
  Dylan and Cole Sprouse / by Amie Jane Leavitt.
     p. cm.
  "A Robbie Reader."
  Includes bibliographical references and index.
  ISBN-13: 978-1-58415-591-1 (library bound)
  1. Sprouse, Dylan, 1992– — Juvenile literature. 2. Sprouse, Cole, 1992– — Juvenile literature. 3. Actors — United States — Biography — Juvenile literature. 4. Suite life of Zack and Cody — Juvenile literature. I. Title. II. Title: Dylan & Cole Sprouse.
  PN2287.S6646L43 2008
  791.4302'8092 — dc22
  [B]
                                                                                        2007000801

ABOUT THE AUTHOR: Amie Jane Leavitt is the author of more than a dozen books for children. She has also written magazine articles, puzzles and games, workbooks, activity books, and tests for kids and teens. Ms. Leavitt is a former teacher who has taught many subjects and grade levels. She loves to travel, play tennis, and learn new things every day as she writes. She believes that everyone should follow his or her dreams.

PHOTO CREDITS: Cover, p. 26 — Gerardo Mora/ Getty Images; pp. 4, 20 — Brenda Song; p. 8 — Ron Galella/ WireImage; p. 10 — Maureen Donaldson/ Getty Images; p. 12 — Jim Smeal/ WireImage; p. 14 — Getty Images; p. 16 — Michael Germana/ Globe Photos; p. 18 — Frazer Harrison/ Getty Images; p. 22 — Nina Prommer/ Globe Photos; p. 25 — Noel Vasquez/ Getty Images

ACKNOWLEDGMENTS: The following story has been thoroughly researched, and to the best of our knowledge represents a true story. While every possible effort has been made to ensure accuracy, the publisher will not assume liability for damages caused by inaccuracies in the data, and makes no warranty on the accuracy of the information contained herein. This story has not been authorized or endorsed by Dylan or Cole Sprouse.

TABLE OF CONTENTS

Dylan Sprouse, Ashley Tisdale, Brenda Song, and Cole Sprouse (left to right) play the lead roles in Disney Channel's *The Suite Life of Zack and Cody*. The Sprouse brothers love performing in their own show. "It's awesome," says Dylan.

Zack and Cody

March 18, 2005, was a special day for twelve-year-olds Dylan and Cole Sprouse. Their first **episode** (EH-pih-sohd) of *The **Suite** Life of Zack and Cody* was showing that day! The twins were a little nervous, but they were excited too. They had worked many long hours memorizing and practicing their lines. They hoped Disney Channel fans would enjoy the show and want to watch it again and again.

They did! Soon after it aired, *The Suite Life* became one of the most popular shows on the Disney Channel. In the show, Zack and Cody Martin live in a hotel suite, which is a group of rooms kind of like an apartment. It's usually very expensive to stay in one, but Zack and

Cody aren't rich. They get to live there because their mom is a singer in the hotel. It's a pretty "sweet" deal, and the two boys definitely take advantage of living in such a fancy place.

Dylan and Cole have a lot in common with their characters. "[They] were originally based on our personalities," Cole told a reporter. Dylan added, "While we were shooting *Big Daddy* [in 1999], we stayed in a hotel for four months and we came up with the idea of twins living in a hotel."

Just like in real life, Dylan's character, Zack, likes to do silly things. Sometimes he gets into trouble. Cole's character, Cody, is more serious. He tries to keep Zack out of trouble. What you see on screen is a little like real life. Cole says, "What's different is, I'm smarter in the show now. Zack is a little more **mischievous** [MIS-cheh-vus]."

Dylan and Cole each have a favorite episode of *The Suite Life*. "'Heck's Kitchen is my favorite [episode] because it was really fast paced and I take over a kitchen, and I love to bake and cook," says Cole.

In that episode, the hotel's chef suddenly quits, and Cody is put in charge of the kitchen. With the help of the other main characters, he prepares a special meal for a food **critic**. As they try to make the meal, things start to get a little crazy. In one part, a squid gets stuck to Zack's face, and the frightened animal sprays ink all over everyone in the kitchen!

One of Dylan's favorites is "Birdman of Boston." In this episode, his brother adopts a baby hawk that flies onto the hotel balcony. "[Cody] has to learn to let it go," Dylan says. "It's pretty sad but funny at the same time."

After appearing in *The Suite Life*, Dylan and Cole became popular stars. They began to make special appearances on some of the Disney Channel's other shows, including *That's So Raven!* And they often sing on Disney CDs.

Even though Dylan and Cole became popular at a young age, they still had to work their way up.

In 1998, Cole and Dylan were invited to attend the New York City premiere of Adam Sandler's *The Waterboy*. The next year, the two brothers performed with Sandler in *Big Daddy*.

California, Here We Come!

Dylan and Cole are **identical** (eye-DEN-tih-kul) twins, meaning they look exactly alike. Some people might even say they have the same face! Yet if you look closely, you can see the difference. Dylan's face is more round. Cole has a small mole on the left side of his chin.

Dylan Thomas Sprouse and Cole Mitchell Sprouse were born on August 4, 1992. Dylan was named after the famous poet Dylan Thomas. Cole was named after another famous person, jazz singer Nat King Cole. The boys are only fifteen minutes apart in age. Dylan was born first, and he always likes to remind Cole that he is the oldest!

The twins are **citizens** (SIH-tih-zens) of two countries. They were born in Arezzo (ah-RET-soh), Italy, so that makes them Italian citizens. Since their parents, Matthew and

Melanie Wright Sprouse is Dylan and Cole's mom. "I can't imagine only having one," she told a reporter in 1999. Melanie has tried to raise her sons with good values. "I'm trying to teach them responsibility," she says. Even at a young age, the boys were doing chores and homework, getting ready by themselves, and saying their prayers each night.

Melanie Wright Sprouse, are from the United States, the brothers are U.S. citizens, too.

When the boys were born, their parents were working as teachers. They taught at the American English language school. When the twins were only four months old, the Sprouse family moved back home to Long Beach in Southern California. Long Beach is near Los Angeles, the movie capital of the world. This turned out to be the perfect place for the Sprouse twins to grow up.

Matthew and Melanie always heard people say how cute their sons were. Dylan and Cole had white-blond hair and sky blue eyes. Their fun personalities attracted people to them. Many people thought the boys should be actors. Their parents agreed. In 1993, when the twins were six months old, they were in their first **commercial** (kuh-MER-shul). It was an advertisement for toilet paper!

Dylan and Cole did a great job in their first performance, and many more **gigs** followed. The boys' acting career began rolling forward.

Dylan and Cole attended the Los Angeles premiere of *Big Daddy* with costar Adam Sandler. "He's a really fun guy," Dylan said of Sandler in 1999. Sandler was so impressed with the twins' acting ability, he told their mother, "[They're] so good it makes me sick to my stomach."

Young Actors

Later in 1993, Dylan and Cole were asked to be in the TV show *Grace Under Fire.* They played the main character's youngest son, Patrick Kelly. How can two people play the same part? Laws will not allow children to work too many hours in one day, so **Hollywood** likes to work with twins. When one twin is working, the other is resting. This way, more time can be spent taping the show each day. The twins worked on *Grace Under Fire* until 1998.

When the twins were seven years old, their matching faces made it to the big screen. They played the part of Julian "Frankenstein" McGrath in *Big Daddy.* The twins must have had a lot of fun working with Adam Sandler, who played Julian's "dad." In 2002 they agreed to work with the **zany** (ZAY-nee) Sandler again on the cartoon *Eight Crazy Nights.*

Dylan and Cole kept playing parts together. They were in *The Astronaut's Wife* with Johnny Depp in 1999. They were guest actors in more television shows, such as *That '70s Show.* After filming *Eight Crazy Nights,* they played the role of Justin Carver in *I Saw Mommy Kissing Santa Claus.*

The twins didn't always play the same parts. Sometimes they got jobs of their own.

Many people think Dylan and Cole both performed the part of Ben in the comedy *Friends,* but it was only Cole. "Dylan would have worked for me as back-up if I was sick or I worked too many hours," Cole said.

Cole played Ben in the television show *Friends.* In 2004, Dylan played Young John in the movie *Piggy Banks.*

Child actors usually have to work all day, while other kids go to school and play with their friends. But Dylan and Cole are more like regular kids. "We went to public school from kindergarten through seventh grade. So, we know what it's like," Cole says.

The only thing that the boys say was hard about acting during this time is that they didn't get to spend a lot of time together. "In the past, when we played the same character, we never got to see each other," Cole says. "One of us would be on the set while the other was in school." They were rarely in the same place at the same time. This was very difficult for the two brothers, because they are also best friends.

All that changed in 2005 when they were cast for *The Suite Life.* In the roles of Zack and Cody, the brothers could work all day together. "It's awesome. We actually get to spend time together onscreen," Dylan said in 2005.

Dylan (right) and Cole have had many positive influences throughout their lives. When asked who their biggest role models were, both boys agreed, "Our family, friends, and our manager, Josh." Josh Werkman, a former New York City talent agent, discovered the boys when they were eight. "I knew that when I met them there was something really big in store for these kids," he says.

Alike but Different

Dylan and Cole not only look alike, they also like similar things. "They love to rollerblade, they like to surf, skate and are into video games. They love animals," said the twins' manager, Josh Werkman. In 2006, the two brothers said they even have the same favorite video game: *Marvel vs. Capcom.*

The twins are very athletic and enjoy most sports. They feel it is important for kids to take care of their bodies. "Eat right. Don't do drugs. Exercise. We like going down to the park to play football or walk the dog," they say. They also like to snowboard and play basketball with their friends.

Dylan and Cole enjoy taking care of their pets. They have a bulldog named Bubba and a goldfish that they won at a carnival. "Most goldfish are two or three inches long, and he's eight or nine inches," Dylan says. They named it Killer because it's so huge.

In December 2005, Dylan (seated) and Cole attended a benefit with skateboard legend Tony Hawk and snowboarder Alexis Waite. Hosted by Sony Entertainment and the Bruce Willis Foundation, this gaming and music event helped raise money for several international charities.

The Sprouse brothers also share similar values and beliefs. They both agree that kids should respect their parents. "You need their rules to organize your life. People always come up and tell us we are polite, and we thank our dad for that," the boys said in 2006.

Dylan and Cole also believe that people should be honest. "A liar is not something you want to be," they say. "It will come back to you." They think kids should look at the positive side of life and be happy. The best way to do that is to get active and help the world around you. "Pick up trash, turn off the water when you brush your teeth." Another important value they share is how they treat others, especially girls. "[Girls] are special. We try to be gentlemen all the time," the brothers say.

Dylan and Cole each has his own personality and interests. For example, Dylan's favorite school subject is science. He likes pepperoni pizza, chocolate chip ice cream, and the color orange. On the other hand, Cole likes English the best in school. He prefers bacon

In 2005, *The Suite Life* was ranked the number one show with boys aged 6 to 14. In the show, Brenda Song (left) plays the role of spoiled rich-girl London Tipton. Dylan and Cole play pranksters Zack and Cody Martin. And Ashley Tisdale plays their part-time babysitter Maddie Fitzpatrick.

bits on his pizza, and he likes cake batter ice cream. His favorite color is red.

In an interview with *Scholastic News,* Dylan and Cole described each other. "He's cool. He's relaxed. He really enjoys getting into something like collecting, and once he has a goal, he will go for it," Cole said about Dylan. In return, Dylan described Cole: "He is actually pretty loud. He's really active all the time and wants to hang out. He wants to have a good time all the time and he's just fun to have around."

A reporter once asked Cole what it was like working with a twin brother. He said, "Dylan and I are on the same tune, the same key."

In 2006, the brothers decided to take their close working relationship to a whole new level. While they continued to work on *The Suite Life,* they also started working on some new business ideas.

It's often difficult for child stars to find a balance between celebrity life and real life, but Dylan (left) and Cole have been able to handle all the pressure just fine. "These kids definitely break the mold when it comes to that . . . ," Werkman said. "They're surrounded by so much support from their parents, their friends, their family and even people in the business. These kids are so loved and so highly regarded."

Young Businessmen

Dylan and Cole aren't the only twins who started out as child actors and made it big. Twins Mary-Kate and Ashley Olsen started acting when they were children, too. As young women, the Olsens started a production company called Dualstar Entertainment Group. In 2005, they asked Dylan and Cole to sign with their company. Mary-Kate said, "They already have a following, so we're really excited to see where we can take them."

By 2007, the Sprouse Brothers already had a line of clothing in stores. They planned on designing other merchandise like video games, CDs, surfboards, and snowboards, too. "This isn't just about clothing," said Werkman.

"It's about lifestyle, it's about products. . . . One of the big reasons for the launch of this platform is that there's nothing for little boys out there."

In 2006, the boys started a magazine, *Sprouse Bros. CODE.* The magazine includes interviews of famous people, and unusual activities going on around the world. The first issue had an article on swimming with sharks in Hawaii. "In our magazine we want to have the video games that are coming out, cool gadgets, **deodorant** [dee-OH-der-unt]. Things guys would care about. We want to aim it towards guys," Dylan says. The magazine also includes a column written by Dylan and Cole.

Also in 2006, they signed a book contract for a series in which they would be the main characters. Cole told a reporter, "My brother and I feel it's really important for kids to read. Now we have a chance to create fun and interesting content kids can enjoy." The first book in the *47 RONIN* series, *The Revelation,* was released in June 2007.

In June 2007, Cole and Dylan attended the sneak preview of Finding Nemo Submarine Voyage at Disneyland. Attending special events like this is just one of the many perks of being a star.

After high school, they both want to go to college. "I want to . . . get a master's or Ph.D in zoology so I can work with animals," Dylan

A reporter once asked the boys what it was like to be so successful at such a young age. Dylan (left) responded, "We have all this stuff rolling now, but we don't get overwhelmed because it's more fun than it is work."

says. He even says he'll give up acting one day in order to achieve this dream. Cole hasn't decided yet what he wants to study in college, but he definitely knows he'll go. "I'm still young and I have a while to think about it," he says.

Whatever the boys decide to do in the future, if it's anything like their past, they'll be successful. For the time being, the twins are just trying to take it easy on their time off, spend time with friends, and in general enjoy life. And oh, what a *sweet* life it is!

1992 Dylan Thomas Sprouse and Cole Mitchell Sprouse are born in Arezzo, Italy, on August 4.

1993 Dylan and Cole appear in their first commercial. They begin playing the role of Patrick Kelly on *Grace Under Fire,* a job that will last until 1998.

1999 They play Julian "Frankenstein" McGrath in *Big Daddy* and as twins in *The Astronaut's Wife.*

2000 Cole plays the role of Ben Geller in the TV series *Friends.* This gig will last until 2002.

2005 Dylan begins playing Zack and Cole begins playing Cody in *The Suite Life of Zack and Cody* on the Disney Channel. They sign with Dualstar Entertainment Group in September.

2006 The first issue of *Sprouse Bros. CODE* is published on July 18. Dylan and Cole sign a book contract with Simon Spotlight in September.

2007 *The Suite Life of Zack and Cody* begins its third season. The twins sign on to star in a movie based on Tom Sawyer. The first book in their series *47 RONIN,* called *The Revelation,* hits bookstores in June.

Filmography

Dylan

2004   *Piggy Banks* (Young John)

Cole

2000–2002 *Friends* (Ben Geller)

Together

2007   *A Modern Twain Story: The Prince and the Pauper* (Dylan plays Tom Canty; Cole plays Eddie Tudor)

2006   *That's So Raven!* (as Davidson twins and as Martin twins)

2005–   *The Suite Life of Zack and Cody* (Dylan plays Zack; Cole plays Cody)

2004   *The Heart Is Deceitful Above All Things* (Older Jeremiah)

2003   *Apple Jack* (Jack Pyne)
            Just for Kicks (Dylan and Cole Martin)

2002   *Eight Crazy Nights* (voice, K-B Toy Soldier)
            I Saw Mommy Kissing Santa Claus (Justin Carver)
            Master of Disguise (Young Pistachio)

2001   *Nightmare Room* (Buddy, 2 episodes)
            That '70s Show (Bobby, 1 episode)

1999   *Big Daddy* (Julian "Frankenstein" McGrath)
            The Astronaut's Wife (twins)

1993–1998 *Grace Under Fire* (Patrick Kelly)

Articles

Carter, Gayle Jo. "News & Views." *USA Weekend*, September 2006.

Mayberry, Carly. "Showbiz Kids." *The Hollywood Reporter,* November 16, 2005.

Thompson, Kevin D. "Sprouse Twins Greet Adoring Fans at G-Star." *PalmBeachPost.com,* November 30, 2006.

Works Consulted

Belz, Leigh. "People Are Talking About." *Teen Vogue*, November 2006, pp. 99–100.

Jaeger, Liz. "Dualstar Announces July 18 Launch of New Boys Magazine, *Sprouse Bros. CODE.*" *BWR Public Relations: An Ogilvy PR Worldwide Company,* July 6, 2006.

Kam, Paulette. "Mary-Kate and Ashley Olsen's Dualstar Partners with Cole and Dylan Sprouse." *BWR Public Relations: An Ogilvy PR Worldwide Company*, September 14, 2005.

Kang, Stephanie. "Olsen Entrepreneurs Branch Out with Boys." *The Wall Street Journal*, September 12, 2005, p. B1.

Keck, William. "The New Twins on the Block." *USA Today*, October 4, 2005, p. 3D.

Picarella, Michael. "Local Brothers Follow in the Footsteps of the Olsen Twins." *The Acorn*, September 29, 2005.

Smith, Kyle, and Maria Speidel. "Daddy's Boys." *People,* July 19, 1999.

Smith, Stephanie D. "Tween Stars to Launch *Sprouse Bros. Code,*" *MediaWeek.com,* July 14, 2006.

"Sprouse Bros. Sign Book Deal." *PRNewswire,* Los Angeles, September 21, 2006.

Telling, Gillian. "Olsens Pass Twin Torch to Sprouse Bros." *Radar Online,* June 26, 2007.

On the Internet

SprouseBros.com: "The Official Website of Dylan & Cole Sprouse"
http://www.sprousebros.com

Disney Channel. "The Suite Life of Zack and Cody."
http://tv.disney.go.com/disneychannel/suitelife/index.html

Scholastic News. "Star Spotlight." http://teacher.scholastic.com/scholasticnews/mtm/starspotlight.asp?sf=sprouse

PBS Kids Go! "It's My Life: Dylan and Cole Sprouse."
http://pbskids.org/itsmylife/celebs/interviews/sprouses.html

Kids' Turn Central. "Meet Dylan and Cole Sprouse."
http://www.kidsturncentral.com/topics/tvmovies/sprouse4.htm

citizens (SIH-tih-zens)—people who are members of a country.

commercial (kuh-MER-shul)—an advertisement on radio or television.

critic (KRIH-tik)—a person who says what's good or not so good about something, such as food or a movie.

deodorant (dee-OH-der-unt)—a gel or spray used to mask the smell of sweat and other body odors.

episode (EH-pih-sohd)—a television show that is part of a series.

gig—a job, especially one for a creative person like a performer.

Hollywood (HAH-lee-wood)—the area in Los Angeles, California, where movies are made and television shows are taped; also, the movie industry.

identical (eye-DEN-tih-kuhl)—the same.

mischievous (MIS-cheh-vus)—behaving in a playful, naughty, or annoying way.

suite (SWEET)—a group of rooms connected together, including bedrooms, a sitting room, bathrooms, and sometimes a kitchen area, generally found in a hotel.

zany (ZAY-nee)—silly or crazy in a fun way.